Learn to Read

Brown Watson

ENGLAND

Contents

Teddy's ABC

"Come with me
And you shall see,
How to learn
Your **a b c**!
Meet my friends!
My family, too!
Each one of them
Will soon help you!
You'll find it's as easy
As it can be,
With us to learn
Your **a b c**!"

A a

"Here I am, at my school –
We have lessons every day.
Is there something on my desk
Which begins with a letter **a**?
That's right! It's an **a**pple!
But, that isn't all –
Just look at the posters
Teacher's put on the wall!
There's an **a**nt, **a**lligator –
And an **a**rk, by the way . . .
An **a**crobat . . . what else
Begins with **a**?"

Bb

"Lots of things here
Which begin with a **b**!
Barney **B**ear in his **b**oots –
And then – there is ME!
B is for **b**ear,
Birds and a **b**all,
A **b**us and a **b**icycle –
Now is that all?
There are **b**elts on our coats
So, just look and see
How many more things
Begin with a **b**!"

Cc

"Picnic time, now!
And the next letter's **c**.
There are **c**ups for our drinks
And our **c**at – can you see?
We eat **c**arrots and **c**ake
And ripe **ch**erries, too!
And **ch**ocolate! Delicious!
Now, let me tell you –
Ch may be
Rather different a sound –
But the first letter's **c**.
Any more to be found?"

11

Dd

"Our next letter's **d**,
Which starts my **d**og's name –
He's **D**anny, the **d**og,
And he just loves a game!
Then there's **D**aisy the **d**onkey,
Another good friend.
She'll never bite
Or try to offend!
See **d**uck and the **d**uckling,
And a big **d**ragonfly –
Any more letter **d** words?
Play a game of I-Spy!"

Ee Ff Gg Hh

"**E** is for **e**ggs,
For a breakfast-time dish.
F is for **f**lowers,
A **f**rog and some **f**ish!
And **f** is for **f**arm
Where my **G**randma, I see!
Her name, of course,
Begins with a **G** . . .
H is for **h**ens,
And a **h**orse eating **h**ay,
And a big **h**elicopter,
Flying swiftly away!"

Ii Jj Kk

"**I** is for **i**ce-cream –
My favourite treat!
Jack-in-the-Box
Would love some to eat!
His name, you know,
Begins with a **J** –
And a big **j**ug of **j**uice
Begins the same way!
Then there's **k** for **k**oala,
My **k**ite and a **k**ing,
And a **k**itten which makes
Knots in the **k**nitting!"

Ll

"**L** is for **l**aces –
One of mine is undone!
A strong **l**ead for Danny –
Every dog should have one.
There are **l**eaves on the trees
And **l**ettuce for tea,
A bright **l**adybird, and
A **l**ollipop for me!
Then a **l**adder for Daddy,
And some **l**etters, too,
Brought by the postman –
Any more words for you?"

Mm

"**M** is for **m**edicine
To take when we're ill –
The **m**oon through my window –
So bright and so still . . .
Then, **m** for the **m**ilk
Which **M**ummy brings me.
And I know there's a **m**ouse –
Take a look! Can you see?
Money and **m**oneybox,
Mushrooms – see them?
How many more things
Begin with an **m**?"

Nn Oo Pp

"Now we are out camping!
Can you see a **n**est!
A **n**ewspaper for Daddy –
That's what he likes best.
Nest and **n**ewspaper
Both begin with an **n** –
There are **n**uts and a **n**et,
What's the next letter, then?
It's **o** for an **o**wl!
And next comes a **p**,
Which begins **p**ath and **p**illows –
Any more? Look and see!"

Qq Rr Ss

"The next letter is **q**
Which begins the word **q**ueen –
Though, here in our park,
There's not one to be seen!
The **r**ain and the **r**abbits
Begin with – can you guess?
That's right! It's an **r**!
And the next letter's **s**
We have **s** for **s**ee-**s**aw,
A **s**lide and some **s**wings!
Look hard! You may notice
Quite a few other things!"

Tt Uu

"Now, the next letter
Is special to me.
Can you think just why?
It is letter **t**!
Yes! **T** for **T**eddy –
Television, too!
The **t**rack and a **t**unnel . . .
Now, the next letter's **u**
Which begins **u**mbrella
To help keep us dry,
When rain begins falling
From clouds in the sky."

Vv Ww

"**V** is for **v**iolin
Which my Daddy plays.
He's a fine **v**iolinist
Doing practice most days.
There's **v**olcano and **v**ase –
Both begin with a **v** –
W comes next –
Through the **w**indow, you'll see
The **w**ell, with the **w**ater
Which is for us all.
Then Daddy's **w**heelbarrow,
Which he's left by the **w**all!"

Xx Yy Zz

"Now, **x** is for the **x**ylophone
I'd like to play!
I had one, you see,
For my birthday, today!
Letter **x** often ends words –
Like si**x**, fi**x** and fo**x** . . .
Then, **y** for my **y**acht –
It was packed in a bo**x**!
Tomorrow, I'm taking it
Out for a sail!
Then **z** is for **z**ebra
With stripes to its tail!"

Aa

Bb

Cc

Dd

Ee

Ff

Gg

Hh

Ii

Jj

Kk

Ll

Mm

Nn

Oo

Pp

Qq

Rr

Ss

Tt

Uu

Vv

Ww

Xx

Yy

Zz

34

Teddy's Birthday Surprise

Teddy Bear woke up, blinking at the sun shining into his room. The birds sang and chattered noisily. Downstairs, Mummy and Daddy Bear laughed and talked together. But why did it feel such a special sort of day?

"My birthday!" he remembered, jumping out of bed.

He hoped he would have lots of birthday
cards, and Mummy and Daddy always let him
open his presents at breakfast-time.
"Happy Birthday, Teddy!" called Mummy
Bear, cheerfully.

"Many happy returns!" smiled Daddy. Teddy said nothing. There was one card beside his plate, but no presents – not even from Uncle Sailor Bill. And he never forgot birthdays!

"Maybe Mummy and Daddy haven't enough money to spend on parties and birthdays," thought Teddy.

He opened the card and up popped a little bear, smiling and waving at him!

"That's your first birthday surprise," laughed Daddy Bear.
Teddy Bear did like the card! He took it out into the garden, opening and closing it again and again.

Teddy was about to go back indoors, when he saw Teacher Bear carrying a basket and two shopping bags. They looked very heavy.

"Do you need any help, Teacher Bear?" he asked, politely.

"Er – no thank you, Teddy," she said quickly.
"I – I think I can manage." And off she went
down the road just as fast as she could.
Teddy Bear was very surprised all over again.

Next minute, the sparrows and robins flew down and began pecking at some sausage roll crumbs on the ground. Teddy knew that they must have fallen from Teacher Bear's basket.

"I wonder where Teacher Bear was taking those sausage rolls?" thought Teddy. He loved sausage rolls!
He was still wondering when he heard voices by the back gate.

It was Honey Bear and Tiny Bear!
"Hurry up, you two," said Honey's mummy,
"or we won't get it all finished in time!"
"Get WHAT finished in time?" Teddy wanted
to know.

But they just went past. Honey Bear's mummy was pushing her shopping trolley with a big box on top. By now, Teddy was sure something was going on, something he didn't know about.

Then he heard voices whispering his name!
"Is that you, Billy Bear?" he called out.
Sure enough, the cheeky face of Billy Bear
peeped out from behind a big tree.

"Oh – er, hello, Teddy," he said. "We were all just going somewhere, weren't we, Bella?" Bella was Billy's little sister.

"What have you got hidden behind your back?" asked Teddy.

"Me?" said Billy. "Nothing!"
He and Bella ran off just as fast as they could possibly go!
"Hey!" shouted Teddy, loud enough for Mummy and Daddy to hear. "Come back here! Where are you both going?"

"What's wrong?" asked Mummy.
"I just don't know!" sighed Teddy. And he told them all that had happened. "Billy and Bella wouldn't even say where they were going!" he finished.

"Why don't we go the same way?" Daddy Bear suggested. "We might find out, then." So, they went along the path. Suddenly, Teddy saw something through the trees…

It was a bunch of balloons, bobbing in the breeze, with streamers and paper lanterns! Then came the sound of a guitar and voices began to sing, "Happy Birthday to You!"

"Happy Birthday, dear Teddy! Happy Birthday to you!" Teddy was so surprised, he couldn't speak! All his friends were there, even Uncle Sailor Bill!

"Mummy had your birthday cake when you saw us!" laughed Honey. "Teacher Bear made the sausage rolls, and Tiny and I brought the balloons!"

"And look at all your presents!" smiled Barry
Bear proudly.
"It's a birthday picnic with games to follow!"
said Mummy. "We will all have such fun!"

"What do you think, Teddy?"

"Well," said Teddy, "I've already had lots of surprises today, but THIS is the best birthday surprise of all!" And, so it was.

Teddy
and Baby Bear

It was the day of the Teddy Bears' Picnic! Everyone in Bear Village had been busy. The picnic food was ready and the playing fields were marked out ready for the games later on. Teddy was helping Barry Bear to put paper cups and plates on a long, wooden table. Soon everyone would be ready for a tasty picnic feast.

"You're such a help, Teddy," smiled Teacher Bear, as she carried bottles of milk and fruit squash to the table. "Could you do a very special job for me? It would be a great help."

"What sort of job?" asked Teddy. "Well," said Teacher Bear, "my sister is coming to help at the picnic, and we need someone sensible to look after her little bear, Baby Boo."

"There they are," cried Teacher Bear, before Teddy could answer. "Hello, Bonny. Hello, Baby Boo."

Teddy Bear blinked. He had never seen a bear who looked quite as sweet as Baby Boo!

"Now, Baby Boo," Teacher went on, "you play with Teddy while Mummy helps with the picnic. You will make sure she doesn't get dirty, won't you Teddy?" Teddy nodded his head.

"Hey, Teddy!" came the voice of Baker Bear.
"Come and help blow up a few balloons."
"Hear that, Baby Boo?" grinned Teddy. "You
won't get dirty if you watch me blowing up
balloons."

But Baby Boo did not seem very interested in balloons. What she wanted was to see what was inside a big flower pot!
"No, Baby Boo!" cried Teddy Bear.
"Don't get yourself dirty!"

Poor Teddy! He didn't see the tin of whitewash Painter Bear had brought to mark out a game of hopscotch on the grass. How Baby Boo laughed to see Teddy covered with big white blobs!

"Here's a cloth," cried Baker Bear.
But Teddy could not stop! Baby Boo was already toddling off towards a big basket of fat, juicy strawberries..."
"Don't get dirty!" cried Teddy.

SPLOSH! Teddy shut his eyes tight. Then he opened them again. He let out a deep breath. Baby Boo was not at all dirty. HE was covered in bright red splodges of strawberries!

Baby Boo laughed so much that Billy and Bella Bear came over to see what the joke was. Then they saw Teddy.

"What happened?" grinned Billy. He and Bella thought Teddy looked so funny!

"It's Baby Boo!" growled Teddy. "I'm supposed to make sure that she doesn't get dirty! Teacher Bear is counting on me!"

"Well, take her to the swings," Bella suggested. "She won't get dirty there."

That sounded a good idea to Teddy. Then Baby Boo decided she wanted a drink at the water fountain. "Mind that puddle!" warned Teddy Bear. "Don't get yourself dirty!"

SPLASH! Baby Boo didn't step into the puddle, but Teddy Bear did! Baby Boo looked down at her clean paws and her clean clothes. Then she looked at Teddy, and started laughing again.

Baby Boo didn't stop to see how angry Teddy was. She had just seen a big tub of sawdust that Mummy Bear had brought for the lucky dip. It was just inside a big tent, and Baby Boo headed straight for it.

"Baby Boo!" Teddy Bear shouted. "Come here!" He dashed into the tent after her. The next thing he knew, there was a shower of sawdust, grass and earth flying about. The tent fell down around him.

He could hear voices outside.
"What's happened to the tent?"
"Didn't Teddy Bear go inside?"
"Teddy? But I asked him to look after Baby Boo! He was supposed to see she didn't get dirty!" said Teacher.

"Baby Boo?" said Baker Bear. "She walked straight past the tent." There was silence. Slowly, very slowly, and with bears pulling and pushing and prodding him, Teddy Bear crawled out.

Nobody knew what to say.

"Teddy!" gasped Mummy Bear at last. "What HAVE you been doing?"

"I've been looking after Baby Boo," Teddy protested, "making sure she didn't get dirty!"

"My little Baby Boo?" said her mummy. "Just look at her! She's kept herself BEAUTIFULLY clean!"

"Yes, but..." began poor Teddy.

"YOU'RE covered with sawdust and muddy splashes!" said Teacher.

"And there's sticky strawberries on your fur!" said Baby Boo's mummy.
"To say nothing of all that white-wash!" sighed Mummy Bear. "Oh, Teddy! On the day of the Teddy Bears' Picnic, too!"

"Wait a minute," said Baker Bear. "Teddy DID look after Baby."

"And he made sure she didn't get dirty," added Barry Bear.

"And there's no harm done," said Daddy Bear.